BRADFORD, EH?

JASON M CROOT

Copyright © 2025 Jason Croot

All rights reserved.

ISBN: 9781068791123

FOREWORD

Jason and I first connected on LinkedIn after discovering our shared Bradford roots.

It was clear that not only did we have a shared artistic drive, which we both pursued with a passion, but also, I discovered that we had lived just a stone's throw from each other in an area of Bradford just off Leeds Road. I learned that his mother had attended the same school I did, St. Peter's, where she later became an assistant teacher. Hearing all of this brought back so many fond memories of my childhood and all the fun times with friends in the playground. Even to this day, I remember the smell of the school dinners that were wafting in our general direction in the playground. The school was close to our home, and I have vivid recollections of walking to school each morning with my two brothers.

BRADFORD, EH?

It makes me smile to think that both myself and Jason would have each held on to big dreams as we ran up and down those cobbled back lanes in our neighbourhood. We will have both grown up experiencing a wealth of cultural diversity with friends who came from many different backgrounds. Those interactions will be amongst the things I'll always treasure, and they have continued to enrich my life whilst grounding me moving forward.

There are just so many reasons to love Bradford. Prior to becoming a full-time musician, I was employed in many different types of jobs, from sewing machinist to clerk typist. A lot of that work took me to various parts of Bradford, and I often marvelled at the huge buildings and mills that highlighted Bradford's industrial heritage. In my late teens, I had a job helping out in a recording studio which was located in an area of central Bradford known as 'Little Germany'. The architecture of the buildings in this area is neoclassical and has an Italian influence. The buildings were mainly offices and warehouses built by German wool merchants in the 1800s. The area often leaves a feeling that you are walking around the streets in a different European country, which adds a further diverse dimension to Bradford.

My career gradually moved me away from Bradford, but one of my childhood dreams was fulfilled when we played at the famous 'St. George's Hall,' a building I had walked past many times, imagining I'd play there one day.

Bradford has given me so much richness and beauty, as well as some challenging times, but I'll always be grateful for all of those experiences.

Love and peace, Tasmin Archer

BRADFORD, EH?

INTRODUCTION

Me: 'I'm writing another book.'

'Another one, what's it about? Hollywood? Cannes?'

Me: 'No, Bradford—my hometown.'

'What? Flat caps and whippets and all that?'

Me: 'Pal, Bradford's got a lot more to offer than that.'

'Hmmm. 'Bradford, Eh? So what's Bradford offered the world?'

Note from me:

The dialogue in this book isn't word-for-word, though what I've tried to capture is its essence. There's a tad of mild language here and there, but nothing too spicy. The facts are as accurate as I can remember and to the best of my knowledge. My memory's sharp, but like most, it's a little peppered when recalling Bradford as it was for me in the '70s, '80s, and '90s.

1 WHERE WERE YOU IN THE '80s?

*Bradford, back in the day.
Photo courtesy of Paul Coupland.*

BRADFORD, EH?

Where were you in the '80s?

I was a teen living in my hometown of Bradford. I, like most teens, went through an identity crisis. From Mod to goth to punk. From having a bleached-blond flat top to an '80s male perm. As Bradford moved through the years, I didn't know if I wanted a haircut or a shite; I changed hairstyles and looks more times than I'd eaten hot dinners.

'You look like a poodle, our kid.'

On weekends, with my ripped bleached jeans, gelled home perm and Hai Karate on, I'd head off to either Time and Place or Dollars and Dimes junior disco on Manningham Lane; these were the places to be. I used to rock my red Campri ski jacket, thinking I was the business, especially when *Take On Me* by A-ha came on. I'd unzip my jacket, letting it fall, hang halfway down my back, and reveal my cool Kappa T-shirt. I'd strut around the edge of the dance floor like a turkey, hoping to impress the big-haired girls clothed in neon and bold dangling jewellery. Looking back, the only person I could've impressed was Bernard Matthews.

A couple of years before that, I found myself in Bradford's Mod scene. Though I was much too young for a Lambretta scooter, I had the rest of the look down: my checked Rupert trousers, my navy blue French-flagged Pod shoes, and my khaki green fishtail parka pinned with Mod and Ska badges, with a target on the back. Needless to say, I was a real victim of fashion, but I felt like the bee's knees. My Walkman was loaded with cassettes of The Specials, Madness, and Bad Manners. I'd cruise around town, wishing for the day I'd be old enough to ride a cool moped, just like in *Quadrophenia* (1979). In the meantime, I had to make do with the number 72 bus. So, rather than London to Brighton, it was Leeds to Bradford for me. *Kerching* a Saver Strip.

Dad and my spaniel Beulah sporting natural curls, and me with my '80s home perm.

Cannon Cinema Broadway in the '80s.
Photo courtesy of the Telegraph & Argus, Bradford.

In the '80s, teens used to bop down to the two local cinemas—the ABC and the Odeon—and queue up to watch films like *Ghostbusters* (1984), *Weird Science* (1985), and *Back to the Future* (1985) for around two quid a ticket. Bargain.

By the mid-'80s, ABC had sold their cinemas to Cannon. It started showing more X-rated films like *Lemon Popsicle* (1978) and *Porky's* (1981). When *A Nightmare on Elm Street Part 2: Freddy's Revenge* (1985) came out, my mates and I were only 14. Undeterred, we tried our luck anyway, hoping to pass for 18 just to get in...

'I need to see some ID, lads!'

Our teenage acne, fake deep voices, and the fact that we were chewing through about twenty sticks of Juicy Fruit each gave the game away. We failed.

'I told you the chuddy wouldn't work, you tosser,' jibed one of my mates before we all carried away our teenage bravados, chanting:

"*Everywhere We Go, People Wanna Know...*" over and over again as we cruised through town.

We were not the only ones busting a tune; Bradford's music scene had something to say in the '80s, and it said it loud. We rocked the world and gave it The Cult, New Model Army, and Smokie, who had been rocking it since the '60s. The bands might've been from different ends of the spectrum, but they all had that Bradford edge: raw, unfiltered, and determined.

BRADFORD, EH?

Music, films and fashion were going through the gears like the '80s classic 10-speed Raleigh Europa.

Raleigh had the best bikes in the '80s: Grifters, Bombers, and the super cool BMX Vektar. After watching the cult '80s film *BMX Bandits* (1983), my brother and I wanted BMXs. Though this was not meant to be, from a second-hand shop on Ingleby Road, Girlington, Mum bought us the second-best-coolest set of wheels on the planet: the iconic red Raleigh Chopper. However, there was one drawback: we had to share. I felt as free as a bird cruising on our Chopper. It was a feeling that could only have been made better if my older brother didn't hog the riding privileges and demote me to riding our Chopper like a back-seat passenger eleven times out of ten.

Odeon Cinema in the City Centre, back in the day.
Photo courtesy of Alan Murray-Rust.

*'80s Breakdancing.
Photo courtesy of John Isaacs (D.J. Junk).*

BRADFORD, EH?

Breakdancing flippin' 'eck

'80s Bradford saw breakdancing crews battle each other as they busted out their best moves as Shannon's tune—*Let The Music Play* pumped out from their gigantic ghettoblasters. My best mate and I had a go at getting into a crew inspired by watching *Breakdance the Movie* (1984). Drunk on cans of Quatro pop and energised with Lucozade Energy tablets, I donned my Gola trackies, Puma suedes, and head and wrist sweatbands. I watched a few breakdancers do their headspins, windmills and turtles on the cardboard stage laid on the ground while Salt-N-Pepa's *Push It* pumped from the ghettoblaster. Then it was my turn, but I got cold feet. My braver best mate, however, was more successful and managed to get into Bradford's Beat Street Boys crew.

As teens with barely any money, my mates and I mostly just window-shopped, spending hours browsing stores like Fit Kit, Sugg Sport, Carters and Sportsshoes Unlimited, hoping to snag a pair of Adidas Sambas or Gazelles on sale. More often than not, we all ended up with the same, cheaper alternatives, like our matching Dunlop Green Flash trainers. We'd window shop at Hargreaves on Upper Millergate, and after peeling our faces away, we'd head off to Jean Junction, dreaming of finding a pair of red-tagged 501s in the sale, just like in Nik Kamen's laundry ad, only to end up with a pair of Easy jeans instead.

My best mate and I were real fashion victims, and we'd heard that fashion hit the South first, both not being great at geography and not realising that the South meant London, not West to Manchester, where we headed off to together with our saved-up pocket money one Saturday. After a few hours and getting lost hundreds of times, we were chuffed to bits to find a JD Sports that sold green Ocean Pacific jumpers with big pictures on the back. They cost a whopping 15 quid. After we each bought one, we headed back to Bradford, ready to show off our jumpers and sport what others didn't have. The following weekend, we went to town, we tied the jumpers around our shoulders (just like the '80s band Haircut 100), we made sure our big Ocean Pacific pictures were showing for all and sundry to see, AND we couldn't believe our eyes when we saw the exact same jumpers for sale in Bradford's sports shops. To make matters worse, every other Tom, Dick, and Harry seemed to have them too.

Back in the day Bradford had some random landmarks in town, like the red giant lips and moving tongue of Gobbles restaurant on Godwin Street, and the giant wooden hippo in the Arndale Centre, where I spent a lot of time loafing about with my mates, riding the escalator twenty thousand times, unless it was out of order, again.

In the Arndale, I remember we could buy a chip butty and a Coke at Littlewoods for a quid. Bargain. From Hagenbach's, we could get the best Cornish pasties or a slab of thick, crusty, French bread pizza for something a tad more exotic.

Arndale had numerous clothing shops like Chelsea Girl, Mark One, and Van Allan, which mostly catered to women. For my mates and me, River Island was the shop that had the pricey clothes we dreamed of having.

Lucy Lockets was where, during my Bros and Wet, Wet, Wet phase, I dared to get my ears pierced. I was glad when the first gold stud was pierced in with all but a sting (a piece of parkin!) BUT...

I wasn't so glad when the second stud was shot into my ear lobe and triggered my mechanism for fainting.

'Stop yer faffin', and get up off the floor, yer big girl's blouse.'

2 BARGAINS, BUTTIES AND BREWS

*John Street in the '80s.
Photo courtesy of Matthew Crowther.*

"Three for a pound! Socks, three pair a pound... Lighters, ten for a pound..."

Back in the day, Bradford was always full of big, bold characters, no frills, no fuss—just straight talk and the unmistakable voices of chancers flogging dirt-cheap goods outside the Aladdin's cave: John Street Market. It was a great place for shops like Bostock's, where you could grab an LP or Cassette for 49p. From one of its few random clothes shops, my mates and I bought our cheaper alternative to the Lacoste polos that we only dreamed of having: Le Sharks. From here, we also all bought five-quid cool shell-satin baseball jackets in the bid to look just like our teen idols in *The Wanderers* (1979).

'But Mum, Mum, it's so big! It's like a tent!'
'Don't worry, Luv, ye'll grow into it!'

Mum was a proper bargain hunter. She'd go to Manorgrove catalogue shop on James Street, or she'd also often wait for the sales at Rackhams on Market Street to buy our glad rags. However, Broadway was the place she loved the most, with C&A being her go-to shop; its clothes were good quality, reliable and lasted as long as its closing-down sale!

Broadway was also where larger fast-food chains had already made their way onto the scene. Wimpy, serving its sizzling burgers, was the first big burger chain to find its way to Bradford town centre. Later, McDonald's and Burger King followed suit. But the big chains and names were the minority, and couldn't compete with the likes of the popular Pie Toms in Rawson Market, where we could grab tasty stand (pork) pies or their smaller brothers, the growlers, which came with mushy peas and a freshly mashed cup of tea all for 80p.

*Rackhams' cafe, back in the day.
Photo courtesy of Matthew Crowther.*

'What can I get ye, Luv?'

Bradford had some reyt tidy cafes back in the day and dirt cheap, too. Some places sold a full English breakfast for a quid fifty, and they were always packed, full of life and chatter. Rackhams' cafe on Market Street was a popular spot after a bit of shopping. Cafes like Fountains in John Street Market, Acropolis on Bridge Street, El Greco on Leeds Road, and Baxandall's in Kirkgate Market were great places for adults to have a natter, grab a scone, and enjoy a 20p brew. My order usually was a plate of chips and a milkshake, which Mum and Nana would treat me to. It was back then that cafes were called cafes, unlike nowadays, where pretty much every *café* comes with an accent.

*Fountains Coffee House, John Street Market, back in the day.
Photo courtesy of Stephen Marland.*

*Fountains Coffee House, John Street Market, back in the day.
Photo courtesy of Stephen Marland.*

Main Street, Haworth. (Brontë Country).
Photo courtesy of Steve Daniels.

Walkmans loaded with Haircut 100, Level 42, and The Communards cassettes, my mates and I would hop on a bus and venture to pastures new, well, not that far, just an hour to Shipley Glen or Haworth-Brontë Country; a hidden gem, tucked away in the Pennines with its cobbled streets, cream scones and tea, and rich history. However, we were not as cultivated as these surroundings; for kicks, we used to photobomb unsuspecting tourists way before photobombing became a worldwide phenomenon.

Kerching a Saver Strip bought—12 bus rides for a quid. Bargain.

I often went to Bradford Library, believe it or not. My favourite book, *The Twelve Tasks of Asterix*, is one of many I remember taking out and one of many I returned late and was charged overdue fines as a consequence.

BRADFORD, EH?

The execution chair in Bradford's National Photography Museum was where, dared by my mates, I'd sit and startle unsuspecting strangers who walked past. I would shake and rock the crazy look as I pretended to be electrocuted. Some shocked passersby who had been watching thought they'd brave the chair after me, and of course, nothing happened.

One Step Beyond

There were a few times when my big brother nearly had my guts for garters...

We both were avid computer game fans, and were lucky to get an upgrade on our Binatone TV Master game and ZX81 home computer to a ZX Spectrum 32k and a Woody Atari. We'd save up some of our weekly pocket money until we had enough to buy second-hand Atari and computer games from SS Audio Video games shop on James Street. Once, my brother sent me off with a tenner to buy the much-awaited cool INDY 500 racing game, which came with a paddle controller. With nothing in stock, I didn't want to come home empty-handed, so I picked up an alternative. Pac-Man? No! Asteroids? No! Pole Position? No! When I arrived home, my brother was (to put it lightly) livid when he saw that I'd bought Atari's Oink! (a three-little-pig game).

'Oink? Oink? Oink? Ye twonk!' He huffed and puffed and almost blew my head off.

The *Smash Hits* magazine, Danger Mouse cans of Cola and a big bag of pick-n-mix I'd picked up from Woolworths on Darley Street did nothing to sweeten his mood.

A few years earlier, we'd pooled our pocket money and planned to buy Madness's single, *One Step Beyond*, and I needn't expand on what he thought when I came home with Worzel Gummidge's, *Worzel's Song* from Littlewoods instead.

Bradford City Centre, back in the day.
Photo courtesy of John Marsh.

I spent most weekends in the '80s watching my beloved Bradford City AFC. (I've dedicated the final chapter to football.) However, when I wasn't watching football at Valley Parade, I would be skating on ice at The Rink on Morley Street about two or three times a week. I never did quite make it to the ranks of speed skaters who raced around the rink to songs like The Cure's *Love Cats*. However, in my eyes, I'd gotten pretty good at ice skating, so much so that I thought myself worthy of using some of my savings to buy a pair of decent skating boots, as I couldn't stand the pain anymore of the blue rental ones that killed my feet. Though I didn't quite develop the skills of Torvill and Dean, I do reckon those blue rental boots are how I developed my hammertoes.

3 TENNER NIGHTS

The '90s kicked off with a bang—Britpop, shell suits, and dial-up internet that took an eternity to load a single page. Music was shifting too, and right there with it was Bradford's own Tasmin Archer, whose song *Sleeping Satellite*, from her debut album Great Expectations, rocketed to number one in the UK. Tasmin Archer isn't just another pop singer—she's something special. *Sleeping Satellite*, with its deep and meaningful lyrics, bagged her a Brit Award for Best Newcomer in 1993, and with a sublime voice like hers, no wonder.

Meanwhile, Bradford's own Terrorvision were tearing up pubs and clubs. *Tequila* was the go-to anthem for weddings, lock-ins, or anywhere folk had one too many.

'Are you coming out tonight?'

'Does a bear shit in the woods?'

First round

Local pubs were always a good place to kick off the night with a sharp livener before jumping in a taxi and heading into town. My mates and I would usually start off at The Smithy on Southgate, which—ironically—always had The Smiths belting out of the jukebox.

Yorkshiremen are known for being tightwads, so a night out with five or more mates always started with wondering who'd get the short straw and buy the first round. The last one to buy the final rounds would almost always spend less. Before entering the first pub, there were serious tactics flying around to dodge buying the first drinks—fastening shoelaces, pretending to have a problematic itchy arse or making a beeline straight for the bog while someone else got the first round in. Once those first pints were paid for and supped up, it wasn't long before, just like in the words of Madonna, we were *Getting Into the Groove.*

Our nights were electric in the '80s and '90s; we were spoiled for choice—Blue Lace, Lingards, 42nd Street, JB's, Tumblers, Rio's, Dukes and Silks, and Cloud Nine were all always packed to the rafters. Weekends meant squeezing into those places, lukewarm pints in hand; we danced on the smoke-filled floors till our legs gave out. *Relax*, as Frankie Goes to Hollywood commanded, wasn't exactly the plan—more like sweating through a night of *Big Fun* with Inner City or losing ourselves to the pounding beats of Black Box's *Ride On Time*. The '80s also gave us the Village People's *Y.M.C.A.*, Damian's *The Time Warp*, and The Gap Band's *Oops Upside Your Head*, the classic down-to-the-floor song and dance.

*Oops Upside Your Head dance.
Photo Courtesy of Ian Calderwood.*

Big hair, spangled dresses, sequined jackets with shoulder pads, leather trousers, silk shirts, linen suits, bucket hats, vibrant leg warmers, and neon tops lit up the dance floors.

'Where did you get that, eh?'

On the dance floor of Cloud Nine, I was once approached by a man who was just as miffed as I was that he was wearing the same one-of-a-kind velvet shirt as me, which we'd bought from the same canny Bradford Market trader. We laughed it off and continued to go our separate ways, partying under the spinning balls and flashing disco lights like the ones that made every nightclub in Bradford shimmer. Revellers like us gave it all we had, along with the biggest pop anthems, like Yazz's *The Only Way Is Up*, which billowed from every club; we danced, we drank, and we were merry till the early hours.

'90s Night Out.
Photo courtesy of Paul Hartley.

'80s and '90s Bradford nights out typically consisted of copious amounts of beer. These, along with club entry, the after-drinking curry at the International, or a doner kebab at Zam Zam's and the taxi fare home, cost just 25 quid or less, with jingle money left over. Incredible.

By the '90s, club tunes had evolved—*Rhythm Is a Dancer* had us bouncing, *Freed From Desire* sent us into another dimension, and *Spaceman* turned every club into a euphoric cosmic frenzy. It was impossible not to move, not to wave our glow sticks in the air, and not to feel on top of the world.

Some Bradfordians will remember the 0898 Telephone Club back in the day. It was a small nightclub just off Manor Row with booths, each with its own phone. Here, we'd ring up a stranger sitting in another booth just for a chat, just for a laugh—and maybe the potential to *cop off*.

Talking of romance, 1985 TV brought *Blind Date* to our screens. In the mid-'90s, it was still pulling in millions. I took my chances, responding to a call for contestants after the prime-time episode had finished. Somehow, after taking a train from Bradford Interchange to Halifax to attend an audition, I managed to get on the show. But I missed out on the love connection and the winner's prize of a trip to the birthplace of foam parties in the Balearic Islands. Still, Maestro's on Manningham Lane soon had foam parties of its own...

After the clubs closed, the crowd would spill onto the pavements and we'd wait for our taxis, saying ta-ra's to a fellow reveller we'd met that night and had a slow dance with, as they'd hand over a tissue with their number written in lipstick swapped in exchange for a promise to call. Then we'd meet up with the mates we'd hit the town with earlier on, if they hadn't left with somebody else already.

Me: 'I'll call you!'

Woman: 'Can't wait, Luv!' (going in for one more kiss before getting into a taxi, which then drives away).

Best mate: 'Ey up, pal, who's your aunty, eh?'

On those great nights out, after having one too many, revellers like me and my mates would blather on about nonsense which we'd barely remember after rising half-cut from our pits (or someone else's) the afternoon after the night before.

'Hmm, what's yer name again, Luv?'

'Ye what?'

Not tonight, Luv, I'm a bit jiggered.

4 BORN AND BRED IN BRADFORD

Nana and Grandad, 9 Sewell Road, BD. 3.

1971 was the year before the last Bradford Trolleybus ran and the year when the stork delivered me to the Bradford Royal Infirmary (BRI), where Mum had taken the Trolleybus to receive her spring delivery.

Growing up in '70s Bradford, the global city, was a cocktail of different cultures. I lived off Leeds Road with my grandparents in a red-brick council house on a cobbled street at number 9 Sewell Road. Our neighbours, the Yasins at number 7, were Pakistani, and the Josephs at number 11 were Jamaican. Our family were a mix of English with a hint of French thrown in for good measure.

My uncle Terry ran the Black Horse pub in Thornton, while my uncle Peter had the Bedford Arms on Wakefield Road. After Grandad, who worked as a hawker, finished buying his fresh fruit at Wakefield Road Market, I, as a young lad, would sit proudly, high up on his shoulders as he'd make his daily stop off to the Bedford Arms for a swift pint of bitter or two to fill his Blakey's segged boits before heading home for tea.

The Bedford Arms was always thick with smoke, full of life, and always buzzing with the clinks of pint glasses and chatter from the regulars. The pub was a haven for flat-capped Yorkshiremen who weren't ones to spend much, except when it came to their toffee-coloured Yorkshire bitter and eye-wateringly strong tobacco.

Every afternoon, men like Grandad would gather in the same corners and swap stories, old and new, filled with their laughter, their swearing and their ee by gums, ey ups, and by ecks. They'd bicker about everything under the sun, between puffs of smoke, swills of bitter and the shuffling noises of their dominoes swirling around the worn wooden tables.

'Champion, Lad, who's tha champion, eh?'

'Ye Jammy bugger!'

Bedford Arms, Wakefield Road.
Photo courtesy of Betty Longbottom.

Around 3 O'clock, customers would finish the last gulps of their drinks and get ready to head home to their teas as my uncle Peter rang the bell and shouted,

'Last orders, Lads!'

Back then, it was typical for pubs to close in the afternoon. Grandad would neck down his pint of bitter before we'd both head off to number 9 Sewell Road, where Nana's home cooking, including sweet apple pie, was always waiting for us.

I was always Grandad's mini companion, whether it was

accompanying him to the Wakefield Road Market, the Bedford Arms pub or just about anywhere that he went. There was once he headed out in his slippers, and hand in hand we went out for the day. Grandad hadn't said a word to anyone. He had taken me down to the newly built Bradford Interchange, and from there, we boarded a train to Manchester.

Note: Passenger steam trains had stopped running in Bradford a few years before I was born. However, there was enough steam from my fuming Nana and Mum that evening to get the trains up and running again when Grandad and I returned to Sewell Road from our secret adventure.

Just one more day of steam-hauled trains from Bradford Exchange.
Photo courtesy of John Marsh.

BRADFORD, EH?

'Where's tha bin? We were worried to bits,' Nana and Mum enquired.

Rather than answer, Grandad burst into song.

"Take me back to dear old Blighty! Put me on the train for London town, take me over there, drop me anywhere, Birmingham, Leeds or Manchester, well, I don't care! (Whoa!) Tiddley-iddley-ighty. Hurry me back to Blighty, Blighty is the place for me!"

Grandad would often drink his bottles of dark ale as he lay on our ageing three-seater sofa, listening to music playing on his favourite vintage record player, eating a dripping sarnie, or a Philip Smith stand pie. Every evening after tea, he would burst into song and sing to me, and then Nana would join in. One of my favourite songs was, and still is, my grandparents' rendition of Florrie Forde's *Take Me Back To My Dear Old Blighty*. I'd often lie on my tummy on our tabby sheepskin rug, spread over the flagged, freezing floor in front of our roaring open coal fire (this was a time just before gas conversion, and fires came in and took up the place of coal fires in homes). The heat from the flames was like a warm kiss to my face as I watched Laurel and Hardy films on our flickering, tiny 16-inch black-and-white portable TV.

From the Yasins' house at number 7, the pounding rhythms of Bollywood films thumped through the walls, mixing with the thick, heady aroma of spicy chicken curry. On the other side, from the Josephs' home at number 11, Bob Marley's *Jamming* played on repeat, and the scent of jerk seasoning curled into our house like a vibrant guest. These strong aromas hung in the air, weaving into the fabric of our street. In our kitchen, Nana's beef stew bubbled away in our oven, the rich, meaty smell battling for space with the scent of crispy Yorkshire puddings, and doozy golden apple pie, which tasted like sunshine on a plate. These were the aromas of comfort and family—these were the aromas of my childhood, my Bradford.

Gas Conversion 1973, Barkerend Road, Bradford.
Photo courtesy of Alan Longbottom.

Leeds Road stars

Back in the day, Bradford was full of lively characters, and Leeds Road was full of stars in the making.

In the '70s, living over on Leeds Road was the very talented Tasmin Archer, a former student of St. Peter's School, Leeds Road. Fast-forward a couple of decades to 1992; she was smashing the pop charts, making her name in the '90s, and leaving a lasting mark on British pop.

BRADFORD, EH?

Living at the bottom of Sewell Road around this time was a young Trisha Brannan, who, a few decades later, gave birth to Zayn Malik, one-fifth of the supergroup One Direction.

I eventually followed a path as a TV and film actor, and though I wouldn't call myself a star, I would speculate that there's something about the spirit in each and every Bradfordian that makes them truly memorable.

It's the same spirit that Polish Anna (Aneila Torba) had. Many will remember her sitting outside John Street Market with her big woolly hat, pinny, and thick jacket covered in badges. The larger-than-life Anna was never without her big stick and a carrier bag. She was always singing and shouting and always bringing life and colour to town.

Anna's wasn't the only familiar voice filling the air back in the day. There were also the familiar shouts from the capped Telegraph & Argus newspaper sellers at the bottom of Darley Street and Sunbridge Road, calling out:

"Telegraph! Get your Telegraph!"

These sounds were as much a part of Bradford as were its whirring mills, frying fish and chips, and local expressions of ey ups, by ecks, and ye whats.

*Polish Anna stencil art by Stewy.
Photo courtesy of Stewy.*

*T & A seller, Darley Street, back in the day.
Photo courtesy of the Telegraph & Argus, Bradford.*

5 PINTS, PRAWNS AND POPPADOMS

'This curry is spot on, our kid.'

Bradford is Britain's undisputed Curry Capital. Every year, there's a national competition to see which city makes the best curry; Bradford has won more times than anyone else. Some say Birmingham and Glasgow are competition, but in my opinion, nothing beats a proper dynamite Bradford curry, which literally blows taste buds out of the water.

'Oof, mi tongue's doin' backflips—can I have some more watter, pal? I'm about to combust like mi dad's Cortina.'

Back in the day, Bradford had a curry shop on nearly every corner, especially along Leeds Road, and curries always excited me for more reasons than one. As a teenager, I'd frequently head to my favourite local curry shop, Pennine on Leeds Road, also known as Taj's. It was home to the best crispy poppadoms, lamb samosas, and unctuous chicken curries that swam in rich, buttery ghee. Here, there was a sit-down 10p-a-game Space Invader parked in the cellar, which I used to play for hours, and then I'd grab a curry afterwards.

Kashmir's curry shop was my second favourite... Kashmir's claim to fame was that it faced Luna Taxis on Leeds Road, which was featured in Andrea Dunbar's Bradford classic 1987 film *Rita Sue and Bob Too*.

Speaking of films, there were an increasing number of households in the '80s renting video recorders from shops like Visionhire on Broadway. And just before the Blockbuster shops burst onto the scene, Bradford had a number of smaller indie shops which rented out three mainstream videos for just two quid.

But Leeds Road wasn't just about films and food—Back in the '80s and '90s, Leeds Road had its fair share of decent pubs too. In fact, around twelve or so watering holes lined the stretch, many serving locally brewed Webster's, Tetley's, and Taylor's beer.

At 18, my local was The Cemetery Hotel where I'd regularly shoot a few games of pool, knock back a few pound pints of Carling Black Label, and drop 50p into the jukebox for five tracks like—*Simply The Best, Caravan of Love, Livin' on a Prayer, Don't Leave Me This Way,* and *Walk Like an Egyptian.*

During the weekdays, the air of male competitiveness filled the relative quietness of the pub as men spent time in the tap room, pints in one hand and darts, dominoes or cards in the other. On the weekend, popular chart tunes were sung by locals, mainly women or some men who had already had a few, who braved the audience of regular pub goers, their jills and pints in one hand and their karaoke microphone in the other.

I'll never forget Les, a regular so off-key he nearly cleared the pub, but no one cared. He had a gimmick, too: shouting, "Thank you" just before the song ended, as if he were on *Top of the Pops*.

'Cockles, mussels...'

'Do ye av crabs?' (Bloke one)

'...Do ye av any muscles?' (Bloke two)

'Aye, lad, I do.'

'Why are ye not carrying two baskets then?' (Bloke two)

(Some punters would joke, and the Cockle Man would smile, probably thinking that was the tenth thousandth time he'd heard those jokes.)

A few times a week, the Cockle Man made his rounds through all the pubs, selling pots and trays of mussels, cockles and pink, plump prawns. I'd always opt for the juicy prawns and drown them in malt vinegar before eating them alongside a packet of KP dry-roasted peanuts, a little *amuse-bouche* before finishing the night off with a reyt tidy curry.

Most of Leeds Road pubs, like The Cemetery Hotel, curry shops like Pennine—Taj's and Kashmir, and the Cockle Man are distant memories, all long gone but not forgotten, but Bradford's love of pints, prawns and poppadoms, I believe, still lives on.

*The Cockle Man, back in the Day.
Photo courtesy of Ian Sheppard.*

6 SUMMER HOLIDAYS 'N THE FIZZ OF POP

*Coach (Sharra) pulling into Bridlington Station in the '70s.
Photo courtesy of Terry Walker.*

Nana, Uncle Peter, Me, Mum, Dad, and my older Brother in '80s, Bridlington.

Many older Bradfordians will remember those first two weeks in August—Wakes Weeks, Factory Fortnight, or Bradford Tide. In the '70s and '80s, half the city packed their holiday gear and headed west to Blackpool or east to Bridlington (Brid). Our family chose the latter.

We followed the footsteps of generations of holidaymakers, jumped on a coach—or a *sharra*, (as I remember them being called) and left Bradford behind for two weeks of sun, fun, and dips in the murky grey North Sea.

Two hours and a few sing-alongs later, the coaches would pull up safe and sound in sunny Brid, fellow passengers would have a whip-round for the driver before stepping off the coach into the fresh sea air. Straight away, we were greeted by wheeling seagulls and barrow boys shouting:

'Mind yer backs... Mind yer backs...'

They would haul our wheelless suitcases on their barrows to our B&B.

Brid was always memorable. It was here, when I was eight, at Bridlington Spa, that I entered a dance competition. I fancied myself as a bit of a John Travolta after watching *Saturday Night Fever* (1977). My efforts seemed to win over the judges. I won!

Snapshots with our Kodak 24-reel camera

Memories of penny arcades, Wendy's Waffles, hot doughnuts, jetty boats and donkey rides still shine bright in my mind of our Yorkshire holidays. These were the sights, sounds and smells of my childhood summers.

My first job as a child was right on the very sands of Brid, where, with my older brother, I worked as a donkey boy and led the donkeys up and down the beach as they carried holidaying children on their backs.

I must've been the youngest employee ever to have been fired from a job. I was annoyed by another bigger boy who was getting impatient with my donkey's pace as he sat on her.

'Make it go faster, will ya!'

The boy did not let up on kicking my donkey, Beulah, despite my repeated requests:

'Please don't kick my donkey.'

I remembered what I had overheard in a conversation among the donkey owners' sons about making donkeys go faster. Of course, I wasn't sure if this was true or not, but I was determined to make the mean boy stop kicking her, so I put it to the test. I dropped a pebble in a tin can and shook it. It shocked me, the kicking kid and Beulah as she sped off like a thoroughbred racehorse, pulling the reins from my hands, leaving the boy bouncing up and down on her saddle, crying for his mummy and leaving me speechless.

It was a great first job until that point, and after being fired, out of camaraderie, my brother resigned too.

Bridlington in the '80s.
Photo courtesy of Leonora Enkin.

There were many topics that sparked an argument between my older brother and me. Both of us were firm with our Bradfordian pride and hardly ever backed down, and this included when we played games.

One game nearly always started off as sweet as pie and ended in a thunderous argument. It, however, wasn't our Connect 4, our Operation, our Top Trumps or our Subbuteo. It was a game of our own invention: Spot the New Car.

Creative made-up games

While in Brid, my older brother and I invented this game, which I think we should have patented when we got a bit older. Because thirty or so years later, the game is now among the millions of downloadable app games of today.

Back in the day, August meant fresh car registration plates. In the game my brother and I played, the first person to spot ten new cars won. Of course, it didn't quite require strategic thinking (like our other games). It always peeved my brother off when I won.

'It's a Y! It's a Y!' I bellowed, legging it towards a gleaming flame-red Vauxhall Cavalier parked up on Victoria Road, just as I was about to confirm my victory—Agggghhh! Down I fell on the corser edge. Face first. Chinos ripped. Pride in tatters.

'Stop laughing, ye berk, it's notttttt funnnnny!!!!'

'Ye dingbat! Ye twonk! Ye wasak.' My brother roared, helpful as always! He stood there, in bits, doubled over laughing as I lay tasting the pavement, wondering if the Cavalier was even a chuffing Y in the first place.

Happy in muck, eh?

BRADFORD, EH?

It was good to have dog days and summer holiday fun, catch that fresh sea air, gorge on sweet treats, and fool around with my brother. But that isn't to say I didn't have fun and sweet times in Bradford.

'Are ye playin' out?'

From racing on our Spacehoppers to playing kerby and footy with my mates on the streets, fun was simple and endless, until our mums would shout. 'Tea's ready, come on, look sharp, it's going cold.' After we'd wolfed down our grub, we'd be out again playing footy until dusk.

We would often try to smooth out disagreements that arose between us by swapping Panini football cards and stickers. My tipples of choice during fun times in those warm childhood years in Sewell Road, Bradford, were Dandelion & Burdock and American Cream Soda Pop.

'Pop van's 'ere!'

Twice a week, pop vans rattled up our street. This is when I'd bolt to the top of the road, clutching empty bottles to swap for 10p each. I sometimes made almost enough to grab a couple more bottles of fizzy American Cream Soda. If the pop van hadn't come around, I'd satisfy the cravings of my extremely sweet tooth with other wonderful local choices of sweet treats.

'I'm off to Khalid's Nana.'

'D'ye av all yer empty bottles, Luv? Don't forget to get the Green Shield Stamps, will ye?'

I'd scuttle off to Khalid's corner shop on Leeds Road. Here, Yorkshire brands like Ben Shaw's and Bradford's own Gee Bee sat proudly on the shelves, among the bigger branded Coca-Cola in glass bottles. I mostly always opted for the local brands, because of their great flavours like Pineappleade and Dandelion & Burdock, and the pull of having empties, which I could also return for some jingle money.

Khalid's had a penny bubble gum machine and stocked all sorts of what we called 'spice' (sweets). Fruit Salads, Popping Candy, Refreshers, Flying Saucers, and Tooty Frooties were delights for children, who would also be drawn to scrummy chocolate bars like 54321's, Trio's and Cabanas. Khalid's was an example of many shops stocking sweets back in the day in Bradford, which were a paradise to any child's eyes, including mine.

The Pop Man and his van, Back in the 80s.
Photo courtesy of David Grant.

7 SCHOOL SCRAN AND THE RENTMAN

"Yellow belly custard green snot pie mixed all together with a dead dog's eye…"

"Milk, milk, lemonade, around the corner, chocolate is made…"

Do you remember your first school?

My first school days at St. Matthew's on Saffron Drive, Allerton, were interesting and memorable.

I remember when my best friend had forgotten his sports shorts for PE, but I was there to save the day as I had two pairs in my bag, one of which I lent to him.

He was as pleased as punch that he wouldn't get in trouble for forgetting his kit, and we both joined our mixed gymnastics lesson, during which we all had to take turns running and jumping over the school's pommel horse. When it was my best friend's turn, I stood with the class, waiting, while he jumped over the pommel horse, which went without a hitch, until my friend landed on the mat. The shorts I'd loaned him fell down and draped around his ankles. I hid, laughing the hardest, behind my other giggling classmates, because I knew when I lent my friend the shorts that they had a loose elastic. Needless to say, the hysteria that this caused warranted a visit to the headteacher's office. This was one of many times that my best friend and I ended up there.

The first time we ended up in BIG, BIG, BIG trouble was when we overstepped our tuck shop monitor privileges and got carried away chomping on the tuck shop goodies without permission, only to be caught!

School Dinners

I fondly remember that even though school dinners had a bad reputation, St. Matthew's used to dish out some decent scran. Children like me lined up keen as mustard, all for a warm piece of mouth-watering cheese flan, sizzling spam fritters, and dollops of buttery yet tangy rhubarb crumble, or whatever was on the menu. I loved most of my school dinners, apart from the custard, that is, which made me gip!

'No custard for me, Miss.'

My middle school, St. Edmund Campion, Rhodesway, Allerton, was a contrast and didn't have the most memorable school dinners, which is why my best chum and I would opt to buy our sandwiches from the Rossi's ice cream van that was parked on the school grounds at lunchtimes and treat ourselves often to an ice cream dinner instead; even in winter.

Our delicious lunches consisted of two marshmallow wafers coated in chocolate, packed with lots of soft vanilla ice cream, strawberry sauce, hundreds and thousands, a 99 Flake, and a fudge finger. All of this (incredibly) only cost a quid.

St. Bede's Sarnie

At upper school, St. Bede's Grammar, Highgate, Heaton, I would dodge the long dinner lines and grab a St. Bede's sarnie from Highgate Fisheries across the road, while most chippies sold teacakes. St. Bede's sarnies went a bit further. No one knew who invented them, but they were legendary. These consisted of half an uncut loaf hollowed out and stuffed with chips; sometimes, I'd have it with fish or fish cakes drenched in salt, vinegar, and ketchup. I'd even stuff the dough back in and soak it with more vinegar. It made do for my fuel for the day.

'Can I av a well-done special and chips with scraps, and a teacake? Luv, ta.'

In my opinion, nothing has quite beaten God's Own County's fish and chips. A long piece of flaky, strong-tasting haddock fried in golden batter alongside fat, fluffy chips, which were fried to perfection before being doused in salt and vinegar. Back in the '80s, all of these were served open in a cone of newspaper. On a good day, a kind chippie would throw in some scraps and additional half a fish (a Jockey) for free.

Bradford had some cracking chippies, and for me, the most memorable ones were Hilltop Fisheries Allerton Road, Banett's, Killinghall Road, Parry Lane Fisheries, Fish Dish on James Street, Tribells on Sunbridge Road and Mother Hubbard's on Ingleby Road, which opened in 1972, famously by *Coronation Street* characters Stan and Hilda Ogden.

Tea time

Now, the names for meal times in Bradford (and up North in general) might puzzle outsiders. As I knew them, Breakfasts were fry-ups, Lunches were dinners, and evening meals were tea, but not to be mistaken for a brew. Later, a meal, if we had one, would be a supper like a fish and chip supper.

'Can I call you back, mate? I'm just eating my tea.' I said.

'Eating tea, what? Are you having a Turkish bath, mate?' replied my puzzled pal (a Londoner) when he rang me up.

I cleared it up quickly, also emphasising that we northerners like to eat our food while it's still piping hot, not chat for an hour in between mouthfuls. Mum's the same. I'll often ring her, and she'll say:

'Can ye call me back in twenty minutes, Luv? I'm just eating my tea and watching *Dickinson's Real Deal*... Tim Hogarth from Bradford is on, I like him.'

Mum, a born-and-raised Bradfordian, often reflects on her childhood days. She attended St. Peter's School on Leeds Road, starting school in 1949, just three years after the School Milk Act of 1946, which provided kids with a third of a pint of milk each day to improve nutrition.

Now, Mum is in her 80s and still lives in Bradford. There must be something in the Bradford water, as her memory is razor-sharp. She recalled a vivid memory of her own school days:

'Each morning, we'd get a bottle of milk, and in the afternoon, the teacher would ask...

"Who wants to take the crate of empties and spare milk to the doorstep?"'

Mum always volunteered and seized the chance to drink any leftover full bottles.

Food was still rationed when she started school. When my grandad, a market hawker, and my nana, a Yorkshire wool mill worker, struggled financially, Mum and her eight siblings got free school meals:

'I used to wear navy blue knickers with a little pocket for my dinner ticket.' Mum said.

One lunchtime, a nun instructed:

"Listen, children, when you've finished, place your leftover food on the plate of the person at the end of the table." Mum took it literally. Thinking the lad at the end had finished. Mum (who was only four at the time) dumped her leftovers on his plate. The dismayed boy raised his hand and said,

"Sister, sister, Alice Croot's put all her slops onto my plate!" Mum got a harsh telling-off from the nun for that one.

Top photo: Prune Park Lane, Trolleybus 16.
Above photo: Trolleybus 16, Allerton Road.
Photos courtesy of Alan Murray-Rust.

BRADFORD, EH?

Allerton BD. 15

When I got a bit older, I moved to live with my parents and older brother on the other side of the city, on Rosedale Avenue in Allerton. Dad worked in the textile trade; Mum worked at Dolcis shoe shop in town and as a classroom assistant at St. Peter's School, and my brother and I were still at school. We lived down Prune Park Lane, which was pretty lush and green and had a great football field in Prune Park, where I'd play footy with Dad and my mates.

Footy wasn't my only form of daily exercise; the hike up Prune Park (going) to St. Matthew's and St. Edmund Campion and the climb up Allerton Road on the way home were killers.

On lazy or wintery days, my brother and I would hop on the number 16 bus, but mostly, we walked. Passing Bradford's famous Seabrook crisps factory, the mouth-watering aromas of those crisp flavours made our stomachs rumble and were so strong you could almost taste them in the air.

My best mate's mum worked at the crisp factory, and we'd often buy boxes of 24 crisps from her for just two quid. Bargain. Sampling all the new flavours before they hit the shops. I liked the Curry, Mexican Chilli, and Tomato Ketchup flavours, but they never really took off, and to my dismay, they were discontinued.

Living in Allerton meant a bigger mortgage for Mum and Dad. Back in the day, the rentman came to our house on Rosedale Avenue to collect the mortgage for the bank. The moment my brother and I saw the rentman marching towards our house, we'd bolt to Mum, who was usually in the kitchen and warn her about our uninvited visitor. Mum would shift the pan off the hob, and we'd all scramble under the kitchen table. Like the big bad wolf, the rentman would knock intimidatingly. With no one coming to the door, he'd knock again but louder. The three of us would stay still and silent. When we finally heard the rentman leave, Mum would let out her frustration on whatever was cooking, often corned beef hash.

Every weekday morning, without fail, before heading off to school, over Cornflakes or Ready Brek with fresh milk from the local farm, my brother and I would tune into Pennine Radio. 235 FM. It was the best station ever. We'd both hope to hear that school was closed due to snow (well, in winter, that is!).

Back in the day, Allerton and Bradford often had heavy snow in winter, four feet deep or more, and being snowed in often meant school was closed. On these magical days, we'd build snowmen and go sledging on makeshift bin liner sledges. But whether or not we got the news we wanted, the real joy was the music and Pennine Radio's cool, catchy jingle, which went like this.

"There's a magic in the music, through the day and nighttime too. You've a friend who'll play your music, and we can bring it home to you. Pennine Radio: When things are getting tougher, we can help to pull you through. You've turned us on, and we'll do the same for you. Can't you hear it, can't you feel it—all around and in the air? We'll give you the music and more. Pennine Radio is what a friend is for! Pennine Radio 235!"

(Jingle courtesy of Steve England).

Even now, when I think about that tune, it brings me back to those wholesome days.

*Gain Lane, 1979. A particularly snowy winter.
Photo courtesy of Richard Thomson (Geograph Project Ltd).*

*Thornton Road, '70s in the snow.
Photo courtesy of John Marsh.*

BRADFORD, EH?

*Westgate, '70s in the snow.
Photo courtesy of John Marsh.*

THE JINGLE THAT NEARLY WASN'T

Radio producer Steve England went to pitch for a jingle package at Pennine Radio. His presentation was so bad that he ended up shutting his briefcase on his own tie. Jeff Winston, the boss, took one look and figured anyone this useless at selling must actually know what they're doing when it comes to jingles. Steve landed the job.

Ready to record the jingle, a vocal group was in place, but there was a snag. The lead singer was feeling poorly. They kept calm and carried on regardless, including the sickly singer. However, mid-take, things took a turn for the worse when the singer could hold back no more. Not only did she throw up in a wastepaper bin, but she also fainted. Once she'd come around, the group had another go, but it didn't get much better. The harmonies were all over the place; some were out of tune, and others were just guessing the notes. It wasn't going to plan...

After days of re-recording and fixing what they could, Steve and colleague Alan finally sent off for the seal of approval, which they received from Jeff Winston. They'd somehow pulled it off. This was the beginning of the iconic Pennine radio jingle.

8 WHERE THE WOOL WAS ONCE KING

Mill workers back in the day.
Photo courtesy of Janice Staines.

School, if nothing else, was character-building. I was no David Hockney or Carol Vorderman to make any sort of artist or mathematician, and I failed many of my exams. As a young boy back then, history was too long ago from my young world for me to appreciate and care about. However, now that I've gotten older, I can look back at Bradford's past and feel a new sense of appreciation.

The Boom Years: Wool and Wealth

Bradford was a powerhouse way before I was born. It had come a long way from being the village beside a ford (river crossing) and home to just 300 folk in 1086, then known as Bradeford.

By 1800, its population had grown to 13,000 and was home to just one mill. In just fifty years, Bradford went from having one mill to 338 by the end of the century, and its population had increased tenfold. Another fifty years later, the number of mills had nearly doubled, and by then, Bradford was processing two-thirds of the country's wool, thanks to the contributions of Irish, Polish, Italian, and German-Jewish newcomers. By 1914, Bradford's wool industry had made it one of the wealthiest cities in Europe.

Lister Mills, Manningham, Bradford, was once considered the largest silk factory in the world; its chimney, which was once said to be one of the world's tallest, towered at a staggering 249 feet. Samuel Lister's ingenuity and ambition transformed Bradford into the heart of the silk industry. Royalty and presidents had obviously thought highly of the produce coming out of Bradford's mills. In 1911, Lister Mills supplied velvet for King George V's Coronation, and in 1974, their velvet curtains were provided to the White House.

Bradford's textile and wool industries also relied heavily on the contributions of people from Pakistan, Bangladesh, and India from the 1950s onwards. Many individuals and families arrived to support the workforce in the mills. Their hard work and skills became integral to the city.

Despite Bradford's boom, it wasn't glamour for most; in fact, it was very difficult, but where there's muck, there's brass, and in T.S. Eliot's *The Waste Land*, the phrase:

"As a silk hat on a Bradford millionaire," relates to the fact that a few folk in Bradford made a few bob during the bobbing boom.

From leaving school to retirement, my Nana worked in the mills, one of which was Raglan Wool Mill. She worked six days a week and juggled her job with looking after nine children; by the time I was born and throughout my early childhood, she was still dedicating most of her working hours to grafting in the mill. I remember her coming home and saying,

'Ay, Jay lad, it's reet good to get off me feet for a bit. They're burnin' like Roman candles.'

Dad had also been a worker in one of Bradford's textile mills, and when my brother and I left school in the '80s at 16, we both did too. Working at a textile mill at 16, to be honest, was pretty hard going. Our mill was one that churned out textiles and rubber to sell to major foreign clothing companies. To this day, I remember the strong stench of rubber that would often leech onto my skin, try to set up camp in my nostrils. It was a pong which would only surrender after a hot bath. In the '80s, immersion heaters for hot water took an eternity to heat up, so to save time and money, our family would often take turns in the bathwater.

'I'm off for a bath,' I'd say.

'Leave a bit of dirt on, lad. We won't be able to recognise you otherwise,' Dad would joke.

At 16 years old, I didn't take myself too seriously and would lighten the hours of working on the windowless factory floor by playing my favourite pop tunes at the time, such as *When Will I Be Famous* by Bros. I remember this being much to the annoyance of other workers, who didn't very much appreciate it being played repeatedly from my portable tape recorder. I never did quite work out how my Bros cassette found its way into a bucket of the mill's specialist glue!

Nowadays, the majority of Bradford's functioning mills are a thing of the past; they remain a significant part of Bradford's cultural fabric. For many from my generation who grew up in Bradford, it was likely that mills were, in some way, part of their past too.

Salts Mill

A short bus ride away from Bradford, I remember using my *Kerching a* Saver Strip ticket to get to Salts Mill. It once stood as the largest industrial building in the world. Built in 1853 by visionary Sir Titus Salt, Salts Mill was a testament to him.

Today, it boasts work by Bradfordian artist David Hockney, which graces the gallery's walls. It's also home to quirky shops and a cosy café.

Wool Exchange

In the city centre, the Wool Exchange, Market Street, which was built in 1864-1867 as a wool trading centre, still stands today. The wool exchange symbolised the wealth that wool brought to Bradford, and though wool trading no longer takes place here, it hasn't lost its grandeur. I remember when it was a flea market in the '80s, when I used to go with Mum and Nana. I bought some cool retro toys and old Victorian coins that I used to collect. Today, it is home to a magnificent bookshop. It is still a gem of Bradford.

*Saltaire: canal reflections. Salts Mill.
Photo courtesy of John Sutton (Geograph Project Ltd).*

One of Bradford's finest buildings. The Wool Exchange, now a bookshop. Photo courtesy of Stephen Craven.

BRADFORD, EH?

*Bradford Wool Exchange,
Photo courtesy of Betty Longbottom.*

TRUE? FALSE? I DON'T CHUFFIN' KNOW!

*Jowett cars in the Industrial Museum.
Photo courtesy of Justine Gardner.*

Bradford Built 'Em

BRADFORD, EH?

Bradford had its own car maker—Jowett Motors. Founded in 1901, it churned out everything from sturdy little workhorses to the sleek-looking Jupiter model. Jowett was designed by Bradfordians, built by Bradfordians, and used by some Bradfordians for delivering food and goods, and for those who could afford them, they were family cars. By 1954, it was all over. Jowett was sold.

Was Jowett Motors sold to a tractor company?

Bradford Industrial Museum

The Bradford Industrial Museum is housed in the former Moorside Mills, built in 1875. Over the years, it expanded and became a museum in 1974, showcasing everything from textile machinery to steam engines and classic cars.

Was Bradford Industrial Museum once a spinning mill before it became a museum?

Secrets Beneath the Streets

Beneath Bradford lies Sunbridge Wells, a network of clandestine tunnels dating back to the 13th century. They've been a quarry, prison cells, air-raid shelters, and—if whispers are to be believed—a smugglers' hideout. Some say the tunnels were used for shifting goods; others reckon it was folk who were being shifted. Rumours swirl that The Beatles played an unannounced set at the Little Fat Black Pussy Cat Club in Sunbridge Wells. Possibly a last-minute, low-key jam before heading to their next stop.

What do you reckon happened in the Wells?

Sunbridge Wells.
Photo courtesy of Justine Gardner.

*Bradford's last Trolleybus—25 March 1972.
Photo courtesy of Alan Murray-Rust.*

The Trolleybus Capital

Bradford had the first and last trolleybuses in England. The first sparked to life in 1911, and when the last one trundled off in 1972, it marked the end of an era. First AND last?

Is that why it's named the First Bus Company?

Paris? Milan? Rome? Bradford!

Bradford's got architecture that could hold its own against Europe's finest. Walking around and seeing buildings like the Wool Exchange, St George's Hall, City Hall, and the grand buildings of Little Germany, you'd think you'd stepped into Florence or Vienna. But the greatness is spread all around Bradford, like the spectacular Cartwright Hall in

Lister Park. Many of Bradford's Victorian splendours still stand today.

Do you reckon Bradford's splendour really rivals Europe's finest?

*Cartwright Hall.
Photo courtesy of Chris Heaton.*

Legends Live at St. George's Hall

St. George's Hall, one of the oldest concert halls in Europe, has welcomed countless iconic moments, some of which remain woven into the fabric of music history.

*St. George's Hall in 1853.
Published by Illustrated London News.*

*St. George's Hall in 2007.
Photo courtesy of Betty Longbottom*

St. George's Hall.
Photo courtesy of Richard Thomson (Geograph Project Ltd)

In the 1850s, Dickens captivated his Bradford audience with dramatic readings from *A Christmas Carol* and *Oliver Twist*.

Is it true that these performers graced Bradford's George's Hall during the following decades?

In the '60s: The Rolling Stones and The Beatles

In the '70s: David Bowie, Elton John with Kiki Dee

In the '80s: Genesis, The Jam, Paul Weller

In the '90s: Take That and Tasmin Archer

9 FROM GOLDILOCKS TO GOLDEN FILMS

*Alhambra Theatre in the '90s.
Photo courtesy of Christopher Hilton.*

No talk of Bradford can be without the Alhambra Theatre. A theatre with history, the idea of the theatre came about from impresario Francis Laidler, known as *The King of Pantomime*. Built in 1913, it has seen legends like Laurel & Hardy and Peter Sellers grace its stage. In the early '70s, I saw Anne Ashton play Goldilocks there, and I still remember that day. The Alhambra is more than just a theatre—it's part of our history.

Sunbeams

Mum once told me about her childhood wish. She had set her heart on being a Sunbeam dancer and performing at the Alhambra Theatre alongside other main acts. For a little girl, this was like a fairytale dream. But after auditioning, she was told she was an inch too tall. However, her older and shorter sisters, Mary and Eileen, made the cut.

A few years later, Mum got her moment and unexpectedly had a taste of stardom. She found herself on the front page of the *Telegraph & Argus* when her photo was taken alongside Lancashire screen legend Janette Scott, who hand-picked Mum from a large group of ABC minors' children who had been at Bradford's Ritz Cinema on the same day as the actress.

Like Mum, I was captivated by performances as a child—whether in film, TV or on stage. My sights weren't set on being a Sunbeam but on the co-starring role in my school nativity at St. Matthew's. However, my weeks of good behaviour leading up to the performance, in the hope of not losing my coveted part, were all in vain, as I ended up missing my own class performance due to tonsillitis. I was replaced by my chuffed chum. A year later, I did, however, manage to win the St. Matthew's fancy dress competition as Captain Hook.

BRADFORD, EH?

1977. Me as Captain Hook on Rosedale Avenue, Allerton.

Drama

In the late '90s, I was down on my luck, unemployed and reeking of desperation. I enrolled in a one-year N.C.F.E drama diploma at Bradford College, costing just £15 for the year. Incredible. Our classes were held in a rundown church hall at the bottom of Wakefield Road. The stage had broken floorboards and a leaking ceiling, but it had character and atmosphere. For our final exam, I performed at Bradford University, marking the start of my acting career, and shortly afterwards, with a drama diploma in hand and a VHS copy of a short film shot in Bradford, which I acted in, I left my beloved Bradford for the Big Smoke.

After a few weeks, I missed Bradford. I missed the fresh air, I missed Mum's comforting corned beef hash and bubble and squeak, and the feeling of home. When I could, I'd go back on weekends to recharge in the place where people tell it like it is.

Bradford Bookshop

'Can you pass me that book, lad? I can't quite reach it. The Harold one, ta,' an elderly stranger asked.

'The Harold Pinter one? Funny enough, I'm doing one of his plays, *Betrayal*, at drama school,' I replied.

'No, lad, I can't chuffin stand him! I watched some of his plays on the BBC and couldn't make head nor tail of 'em! The Harold Robbins one, ta.'

As I flicked through the shelves that day, I realised just how many writers Bradford had given the world, and J.B. Priestley was one of them. He was the man behind An *Inspector Calls* (1954). He was a man that Bradfordians thought enough of to make a statue of him, which stands in Bronze outside the National Media Museum in Bradford centre. Then there's the Brontës. Charlotte, Anne, and Emily were all born in Thornton, Bradford, and were the genius Bradfordians behind the world's literary classics, like *Jane Eyre* by Charlotte, *Wuthering Heights* by Emily and *The Tenant of Wildfell Hall* by Anne. They didn't just write books; they were among those who set the precedent for greatness.

From Comedy to Hollywood

Besides literature, Bradford has a knack for producing comedy and great actors. Rodney Bewes, the face of *The Likely Lads* (1964), brought wit and charm to British TV. A few decades before this, Pat Paterson, a Bradford lass, cracked Hollywood and starred in *Charlie Chan in Egypt* (1935) and *Idiot's Delight* (1939). Adrian Edmondson was another gifted Bradfordian and one of the stars of The *Young Ones* (1982) and *Bottom* (1991), which turned pure and utter chaos into TV art.

Lights, Camera, Bradford

Bradford had its fair share of limelight appearances in film. The IMAX theatre, opened in 1983, was the first IMAX to be opened in Europe. Bradford was the world's first UNESCO City of Film in 2009, beating off hot nominees like Los Angeles, Cannes, and Venice. Bradford, with its grand Victorian buildings and palpable northern grit, made the perfect film location for *Peaky Blinders* (2013), *Happy Valley* (2014), and *The Crown* (2016).

Bradford also made appearances in the classics. *Room at the Top* (1959) based on the novel by John Braine (a fellow former student of St. Bede's Grammar). The film won two Academy Awards. *Billy Liar* (1963) nailed Northern humour and ambition, and *The Railway Children* (1970) turned Oakworth Station into a film location —later revisited for scenes in *Pink Floyd: The Wall* (1982). Some big hitters also hit Bradford, such as Richard Gere and Vanessa Redgrave, who starred in the drama film *Yanks* (1979).

Then there's *Elevator Gods* (2025)—Bradford's answer to The *Commitments* (1991). Filmed in Bradford and York in 2018, directed by my mate and Yorkie Pete Hunt, one of the main characters was played by me.

*Cobra (Me) and Socket (Stuart Wolfenden) on the
Elevator Gods Set.
Photo courtesy of Pete Hunt.*

10 THAT'S MAGIC OUR BRADFORD

I remember that as a boy, I loved toys and loved Carters toy shop on the junction of Market Street and Bridge Street. It was a child's paradise, a Tardis of toys and games that could feed most children's imaginations. Every time I went to town with Mum or Nana, I remember wanting to go there and marvel at the Star Wars toys, Subbuteo teams and the Scalextric cars.

In the '80s, I sometimes spent some of my pocket money buying joke and magic trick toys from The Joke Shop in Kirkgate Market.

Testing them out on my unsuspecting school chums.

'Ow, my finger, ye nobhead!'

'Stop yer beefin'.'

I could spend hours rooting around The Joke Shop, spoilt for choice of what to buy, from there I bought things like, nail through finger, jumping beans, snapping chewing gum, electrocuting hand shakers, a red rubber fart cushion and a vanishing coin magic box. Despite my enthusiasm and Abracadabra's, one, two, threes, no magician I would be!!!... However, another couple of Bradfordian lads would.

Master Illusionist

First up, we have Shahid Malik, who began with card tricks and magic. His passion for the art form started at the age of 12, growing up in Great Horton, Bradford. As an adult, his first paid performance was at a club in Allerton, but that was just the beginning. What started as a dream soon became something much bigger. Before long, Shahid was performing on TV, leaving audiences in awe with illusions that defied explanation, such as vanishing coins and watches that reappeared on the wrists of stunned strangers. His talent took him around the world, performing in places like Las Vegas, Dubai, and Tokyo. Yet, no matter where he and his wife and magician's assistant Lisa, travelled, his love for Bradford never faded.

"We love staying at home. We've been halfway around the world, but after all the hard work setting up the show, we love coming back here to relax. We're not into after-show parties and cocktails; we prefer a normal life." — Shahid Malik.

Steven Frayne, formerly known as Dynamo.

Next up, we have Steven Frayne. Like me, Steven owes a lot to his grandad. His grandad was a huge inspiration in his life. It was he who taught him magic tricks in his early days and inspired his love and passion for magic.

Growing up on Bradford's Delph Hill Estate in Wyke, Steven honed his skills as a young lad, eventually becoming a global magic sensation. As Dynamo, he starred in *Dynamo: Magician Impossible* (2011).

'What?' 'Wait!!!' 'No way!' 'But how?'

Leaving viewers gobsmacked with stunts like walking across the River Thames and levitating in front of crowds in Rio. His feats often made people question reality itself.

"Bradford has been overlooked and underestimated for so long–it's now our time to shine."—Steven Frayne.

'Another pair, eh?'

'Aye lad, these were adopted Bradfordian lads, you know?'

Bradford Magic Circle

The Bradford Magic Circle was founded in 1948 by Indian magician Hassan Noor, who had settled in the city. Thirteen people attended the first meeting on Fountain Street, starting a tradition of magic in Bradford.

One of the Magic Circle's most notable members was former Bradford Textile student David Berglas, whose family ran their textile business in Crown Point Mills, in Wyke. Berglas became a leading figure in British magic. In 1954, he hosted *Meet David Berglas* on the BBC, watched by over 19 million viewers. A year later, he presented the first TV magic series in the UK.

And while we're talking about magic, let's not forget about the magic that is produced through art and brilliant artists, namely, Bradfordian David Hockney.

"When I was a boy in Bradford, my mother used to say the world is bigger than Bradford. I now know that to be true, but I like Bradford very much." — David Hockney.

Even long before these Bradfordian greats were apples in their parents' eyes, magic and imagination stemming from Bradford were hitting the headlines. In 1917, two young Bradford lasses, Elsie Wright and Frances Griffiths, convinced the geniuses and experts of the time, including Sir Arthur Conan Doyle, that fairies were real. They'd staged photos and had the world fooled for decades that there was such a thing as Cottingley Fairies.

"Who needs AI when you've got Bradfordian creativity"—Jason Croot.

The Magic of Bradford

Leaving Bradford in 2001 showed me just how much the city is woven within me. London had all the lights, noise and razzmatazz, but to me, it wasn't a patch on home. Bradford stayed with me no matter how far I went. Anyone who, like me, has ventured out of the city will know what I mean. It's in the way we talk, the way we carry ourselves, the way we say it as it is. It's that Bradford magic that you can't quite fully explain, but you just know. You can take the lad out of the city, but you can't take the city out of the lad.

11 A BIT OF A DO

'Come on, Luv, get up and have a boogie with me.'

I come from a massive family—eighteen aunties, eighteen uncles, and well over fifty cousins. With a clan this size, you can imagine the number of Do's we went to in the '70s, '80s, and '90s. Name an event, and an occasion, and most probably, there'd be a Do for it (weddings, birthday bashes, fancy dress parties, anniversaries, welcoming Aunty Anne home from toe surgery). Any excuse, really, for a buffet, a boogie, and a few bevvies.

The food? Classic. A *Smörgåsbord* of Chicken legs, spam sarnies, vol-au-vents, Fox's Party Rings, Black Forest Gateau, Scotch eggs, pork pies sweating under the disco lights, and cocktail sausages that every snotty-nosed kid had manhandled before I got to them. At every Do, there was always plenty of food for people to gourmandise on.

Drinks? Babycham, Pimm's, or Carling. There were always tons,

tons, and tons more beer than anything else. Even though I was underage, I'd drink beer. Well, a 0.01% bottle of shandy to try and look older than I was. Sometimes, I managed to snag a sneaky sip or two of Dad's or an uncle's pint when they weren't looking (or pretended not to see).

And the soundtracks? DJs were pumping out bangers like *Come On Eileen, Tainted Love, Hi Ho Silver Lining,* and *Dancing Queen.*

'Come on, Luv, get up and have a boogie with me.'

I fancied myself as a bit of a Leroy Johnson after watching the TV series *Fame* (1982). I even backed it up with some GOLD medals, albeit plastic gold-coloured ones—first a medal from Bridlington Spa aged eight, then another from Benidorm Palace when I was sixteen. So when my aunties pulled me up on the dance floor at Do's, I was more than willing to join them. *The Loco-motion* and the Conga were always well-received by everyone.

Most of you will have seen 'Dad Dancing,' where all the older men tried and often looked like discombobulated chickens boogying. My dad, however, was a different breed. He loved to wet his whistle, and plenty of beers later, as the night went on, he'd tie his tie around his head, rip his shirt open, and launch himself into full Duran Duran mode. *Wild Boys* was his track. Auntie Mary's Christmas party was where Dad's dance went a bit wrong. As *Wild Boys* pumped out of the Hi-Fi, Dad jumped in the air and made a fake header straight into her prized chandelier. It crashed down, sending glass everywhere, while Dad just lay there, arms spread, like he'd scored the winning goal in the FA Cup final at Wembley.

Ay-ya Ay-ya Conga.
Photo courtesy of Anne-Lise Heinrichs.

Then there was cousin Peter Horne's wedding. One of Peter's mates was away on holiday and missed the Do. When he got back, he watched the camcorder footage and asked:

'That looked like a right good Do. Can I hire that act? He's fantastic!" only to be told the 'act' was none other than my dad in full party mode.

Albert, the Alligator at the Christmas Do

During Dad's Christmas work Do in Idle at The Baron Hotel on Highfield Road, which was a swanky place, Dad did his normal tie-around-head-shirt-off party piece, but the reserved management didn't take kindly to his *Wild Boy* antics.

As Dad trod on their last straw, they warned him to button up or leave. Dad began to leave initially with his tail between his legs, but not before lugging with him the tail of the hotel's eight-foot rubber Alligator Albert he'd nabbed from the foyer. He dragged Albert halfway down the venue's drive onto the main road before the police caught up with him. Luckily, the policeman on duty that night was full of Christmas spirit, saw the funny side, and helped Albert find his way back home.

Dad and Mum at a Bradford Do.

12 BRADFORD, WHERE LEGENDS ARE MADE

Photo courtesy of Paul Sherratt.

BRADFORD, EH?

Thanks a lot, or ta, as we say in Bradford, for sticking with me till the end. *Kerching* a Saver Strip done, we're at the last stop, and nearly there, but I just couldn't finish this book without mentioning football, my journey and my affection for my home team club, my beloved Bradford City AFC. I know football isn't everyone's cup of tea, but hopefully, even if you're not a fan, you'll stick with me for the next few pages. No worries if you fancy hopping off here and scrolling or flicking ahead a bit.

In the early-mid '80s, I'd juggle between going ice skating and my other love of watching City play. Did we always win? Nah, did we 'eck, but we had some cracking players—Ces Podd, Peter Jackson, Trevor Cherry, Greg Abbott, Mark Ellis, John Hendrie, Stuart McCall, Bobby Campbell and the super fast, Don Goodman.

The joy of 1985's promotion was unforgettable, but that same year brought tragedy. On the 11th of May, the Bradford fire claimed 56 lives, all of whom will never be forgotten. I wasn't at the game, but I'll never forget the smoke that covered the City. Bradford grieved, but the Club, City Players, the Fans and all Bradfordians Stood Together. By the next season, we were up a division, playing home games at temporary stadiums like Leeds Road, home of Huddersfield Town; Elland Road, home of Leeds United; and Odsal Stadium, home of Bradford Northern (now Bradford Bulls).

While City waited for Valley Parade to be rebuilt, new faces like the talented Karl Goddard (I loved his skills, especially the *Cruyff Turn*) and Leigh Palin joined the journey.

Watching City was my dopamine, I followed City home and away, alongside the other loyal City fans, often standing in the uncovered away ends, drenched to the bone in non-stop driving rain in autumns or freezing our nuts off in minus-degree winters. Our spirits were never dampened. Well, most of the time, that is.

"PENALTY!!!! Friggin 'ell, Ref, What yer playing at? Where's yer bleeding glasses, eh?"

I loved watching City, especially at home games. The clicking of the turnstiles, stepping onto the Kop, and drinking in the electric atmosphere at Valley Parade filled every corner of my soul. That fantastic surge of excitement when the City players came onto the pitch was something else. The unexpectedness, the anticipation and the incredible sound it made when one of the City players' boots clouted the ball, and you knew, you just knew it was going to rip the back of the net; that sensation was like sunshine in the rain.

"We love you, City, we do, We love you, City, we do, Oh, City, we love you.."

As we stepped it up a gear in the late '80s, we City fans dared to dream that the big time was near.

Bradford City vs Derby County at Valley Parade in 1982.
Photo courtesy of Steve Daniels.

BRADFORD, EH?

"Terry Dolan's, Bradford army. Terry Dolan's, Bradford army..."

I attended all but three games, home and away, in the 1987-88 season; the *nearly season.*

City had a real spirit and a real togetherness; they were playing with heart, and they were playing like champions. City fans and I dreamed of watching City in the top flight, going to stadiums like Old Trafford, Anfield, and Highbury Stadium, playing against Manchester United, Liverpool, and Arsenal. It would've been a big step up from the days of taking a coach down to Portsmouth, Wimbledon, or Plymouth Argyle.

'Jason, what time do ye call this, eh? Ye know ye won't get up for work in the morning... av ye been drinking?'

'Nah Mum, been to watch City...' (We'd won 5-1 away at Fulham, so I was drunk on happiness).

'...Get to bed, Jason, and no playin' video games, do ye hear me...'

'Yes Mum, NO mum...'

The double-deckers down the M1 and M6 on away games in the '80s and '90s were always memorable; playing cards, having a few cans of beer and sing-alongs. Midweek games could sometimes see you not get home till way after midnight, and I'd get an earful from Mum. It was great to see City win away, and do the Conga while singing:

"Jingle bells, jingle bells, jingle bells all the way, oh what fun it is to see City win away, hey."

BRADFORD, EH?

It was great when we won, but it was a long way home when we'd lost, especially matches in London or on the South Coast, but as the chant went: *"We will follow the City, over land or sea to victory."*

We all believed we could achieve the dream and watch City in the top flight. Just to think that City was playing in Division Four in 1982, and now, six years later, they were looking to hit the big time. One game I'll never forget in the 1987-88 season was away at Stoke, City won 2-1, and Mark Ellis scored a 35-yard screamer. It was such a great goal which tattooed itself onto my mind. On a night out, I bumped into Mark Ellis, having already had one, two or maybe a few pints; I tangoed my way over to him.

'Hello, hmmm, Mark, I'm Jay, a City fan, hmmm, I just want to tell you that I saw your goal at Stoke, and hmmm, it was one of the best I have ever seen...'

He shook my hand, and it made my year.

As City sailed through the 1987-88 season, the Bee Gees *You Win Again* played over the speakers at Valley Parade. We had Paul Tomlinson (Tommo) in goal, which gave us nervy City fans a bit of calm. At the back were lads like Dave Evans and Karl Goddard, solid as stone, while Brian Mitchell and Lee Sinnott weren't afraid to get stuck in when it mattered. Our midfield was the heartbeat: Stuart McCall, tireless and fearless; Mark Ellis, who could whack one in from 30 yards like it was a tap-in; and John Hendrie, silky smooth. And up front—Futcher, Leonard, and Ormondroyd—were banging in goals left, right and centre, with nine unbeaten games near the start and nine unbeaten near the end, giving all of us City fans belief and, of course, some bragging rights.

City fan in his local:

'We are going up this year, pal!'

Leeds fan mate: 'No chance, I'll bet you a fiver you don't.'

City fan: 'You're on!'

It was all going to plan, and City still had enough class and enough in the tank to cross the line, most of us thought... That was until City lost their last two games and missed out on going up by one point. Gutted! But we had a chance in the playoffs: City vs Middlesbrough. We won 2–1 at home, thanks to goals from Goddard and McCall. The game at Middlesbrough on the 18th of May, when we lost 2-0, made my heart crash. City players gave their heart and soul and all they had; it just wasn't meant to be. I was 17, and crying in front of other City fans wasn't an option, but when I got home, I shed a puddle of tears.

The following seasons weren't quite the same. City sold John Hendrie to Newcastle, Ian Ormondroyd to Villa and Stuart McCall to Everton.

"STUART...STUART...STUART..."

It was a long wait, but ten years later, in 1998, number 4—my hero and a hero to all City fans—returned. Stuart McCall was back, signed by manager Paul Jewell from Rangers. The admiration and respect we City fans had for Stuart were unmatched. He wasn't just a player—he was the catalyst and the heartbeat of the team. When he played, we believed.

The 1998-99 season was a real scrap—One win from the first six games. This wasn't going too well, but we all believed that we could achieve with the class and quality of the team, with the likes of Peter Beagrie, Lee Mills, Robbie Blake and Captain Stuart McCall.

BRADFORD, EH?

City fan in his local:

'I bet you a tenner City go up this year, pal!'

Leeds fan mate: 'No chance! You're on. Oh, by the way, you still owe me a fiver from the last bet!'

There came many wins, some losses, and draws that felt like defeats... It went down to the wire. On the final, nail-biting day, a 3-2 victory away at Wolves finally took us to the lofty heights of Mount Olympus—the Premier League. Seventy-seven years after City were last in the top flight, it was our time. We all bathed in the glory. If someone could've bottled the euphoria, they'd have made millions.

Chants of "We are going up, we are... we are going up" echoed proudly through the city streets, as gleaming smiles lit them up.

When McCall left in '88, we fell short—one point off promotion. Ten years later, he came back with a point to prove, and he did: we went up by a single point.

City played in the top flight for two seasons, but it wasn't a breeze. The first season went down to the wire to stay up; in the final game at Valley Parade, David Wetherall's goal gave City a crucial win against Liverpool.

City's time in the Premier League was undoubtedly their modern-day peak—and its greatest triumph. It's something all City fans can be proud of. But before Paul Jewell led City to the top flight, let's not forget eighty-eight years earlier in 1911, when the FA Cup—made right here in Bradford at Fattorini & Sons—was lifted by City at Old Trafford, with captain Jimmy Speirs scoring the winning goal. The original cup was stolen in 1895 in Birmingham. For 16 years, winners received replicas.

BRADFORD, EH?

Football ran in my family. My great-uncle John sold chocolates at Valley Parade back in 1911.

Fast-forward a few decades, my cousin Peter Horne headed the youth development at Valley Parade for sixteen years, working with young players like Fabian Delph and Tom Cleverley.

In the '90s, I was playing in the Bradford Sunday Alliance Division Two, and my team, The Bolton pub, Bolton Road, had a pre-season friendly game against Drum Rovers Clayton from Division One. Peter, who had ties with Drum Rovers, came to watch the match... By the start of the season, I was a Drum Rovers player. Peter came to watch me a few times. He was always encouraging, and we'd chat at halftime while I munched on my slices of muddy orange. Peter nicknamed me *'Baggio'*—after the Italian striker Roberto Baggio. Though, in truth, it probably had more to do with my *divine ponytail* hairstyle than my divine footballing skills.

Dennis Croot, top left, with the Slingsby United team.
Photo courtesy of the Telegraph & Argus, Bradford.

BRADFORD, EH?

My dad was a real footballer. He played in the County League, making the pink *Sports Argus* pages regularly for banging in goals. He later managed Slingsby United, who won the Yorkshire County Cup. Dad even had a shot at a Blackpool F.C. trial but missed out.

Even though I never made my school football team, like most lads growing up, I dreamt of donning my team's shirt and scoring the winning goal in the FA Cup for City. I remember as a young lad watching *Match of the Day,* dancing to the tune with my grandad, dreaming of magic football moments, and imagining what it would be like to be in the boots of great players.

It was in the '90s on the turf of Valley Parade, where Bradford's football legends had stood and sweated. At 19 years old, in front of a crowd of nearly 6,000, I tasted my football victory.

The game? Bradford City vs Cambridge United, the 15th of December 1990, League Division Three.

I ran on the pitch, my heart pounding. This was to be MY football moment... I took a deep breath, sized up the keeper and took a run-up.

AND...

Gooooaallll! Back of the net! Speirs, Bannister, Campbell, now CROOT!

What a feeling when the ball ripped the net! I was as hungry as a wolf and felt drop-dizzy when the second goal went in, and then match ball time, HATRICK third.

All those hours of practising with Dad and mates in Prune Park were paying off...

I wiped the muddy leather casey with my sleeve, placed it on the spot, took a run-up... Painstakingly wide. Bollocks!

However, I didn't have time to wallow in my sorrows as time was ticking on. I knew I could do it; I knew I could make my last kick count... I finished strong. I hammered in a fourth—well, toe-poked it in. As a lad who dreamed of scoring goals in front of fans, these were not any old fans but Bradford City fans. No words could sum up what it felt like to score four chuffing goals at Valley Parade...

This was not my debut playing as part of the Bradford City team, nor was it a trial to even get close to being part of it.

My magic moment on the pitch of Valley Parade came from winning the halftime raffle. When my number was announced over the stadium's loudspeaker (wearing my navy blue boating shoes and no socks), I bolted down The Kop just like a contestant from *The Price is Right*.

Before I burst onto the pitch, the organisers gave me a pair of size eight football boots. Even though I was size ten, I didn't let this minor detail detract from this shining moment, although my hammertoes would beg to differ. I had ten minutes and five penalty kicks at halftime at the Bradford City vs Cambridge United game. The win did not stop there. I also bagged a Chinese meal for two, with the main prize being a trip to watch England vs Argentina at Wembley Stadium in 1991.

Winner winner chicken dinner...

'Did I tell you about the time I was on the pitch in front of the Kop?'

'Bit old for a ball boy, aren't you?'

It was certainly a story to tell my mates a bajillion times, or any City fan I got chatting to over a couple of pints of Carling at the Belle Vue Hotel before we headed down to Valley Parade for the match.

BRADFORD, EH?

Later that year, I also managed to get tickets to meet the City players and manager at a function in the VIP lounge at Valley Parade. Holding onto what was my third pint, I spotted City's manager, Frank Stapleton.

In true Bradford style (if you don't ask, you don't get), as bold as brass, I waltzed over to him and went for it.

'Alright, Frank? I'm a striker. Any chance of a trial?'

He took one look at my pint and smiled.

In true Bradford style (you say it as it is), Frank Stapleton said it as it was.

'Maybe if you quit those, we'll see.'

Frank. But fair.

On the Valley Parade pitch, back in the day. 15th December 1990.

BRADFORD, EH?

Looking back, it wasn't just the wins, the goals, or the matches that stayed with me. It was who I was with, the banter we had, the shared heartbreak, and hope. Supporting City taught me how to stick by something when it gets tough, it taught me camaraderie and patience, and it taught me that dreams do really come true.

"What is the city but the people?" — William Shakespeare

People can say owt they want about Bradford, but they'll never take away the memories of our past. There's nowhere in the world quite like Bradford.

So next time someone asks:

'What's Bradford done for the world, Eh?'

Tell them this:

It gave the world stories.

It gave the world art.

It gave the world music.

It gave the world wool.

It gave the world films.

It gave the world food.

It gave the world football.

It gave the world sport.

It gave the world history, and it gave the world culture.

Bradford's given the world plenty.

But most of all, it has given the world its raw, honest heart.

Telegraph and Argus

Who was regarded as Bradford City's greatest-ever player, playing 395 games and scoring 52 goals?

Yorkshire Post

Who is Bradford City's best-ever captain? He gained 85% of the City fans' votes

Width of a Post

Who was voted the Most Popular Bradford City Player of All Time?

None other than...

PTO

BRADFORD, EH?

You guessed it, none other than Stuart McCall.

The photo comes courtesy of the Telegraph & Argus, Bradford, and shows Stuart, celebrating City's 1999 promotion.

AFTERWORD

I first joined City as a young, excitable 16-year-old back in the Summer of 1980, and although I never lived in Bradford during my on/off connection with the club stretching over 40 years, I enjoyed many memorable nights out in the city celebrating victories and a couple of promotions along the way.

Back then, Bradford was a vibrant city with a varied and popular nightlife. Living between Leeds and Bradford (Farsley), we would usually head into Leeds on a Saturday night and always end up in Bradford with its brilliant choice of clubs before the clock struck midnight!!

Although born and bred in Leeds, living a corner kick away from Elland Road as my Dad played for them, City were to become my club in the years ahead and still holds now a special place in my heart and always will.

As a young team in the main, we forged a real strong bond with our

BRADFORD, EH?

loyal and committed fan base, one minute we'd be celebrating a last minute Mega (Mark Ellis) winner at Rotherham with them behind the goal, knowing in a few hours time we'd be singing and dancing with them in the bars of Bradford!

I have so many fantastic memories of the club, city, and people of Bradford and one horrible, tragic memory of the disaster on the 11th May, which is always honoured and remembered at a memorial each year as the city comes together to respect lost and injured loved ones.

I will always feel humble and honoured to be a part of Bradford City, and the warm welcome I always receive on returning, my love for the club started as a young pup and is as bright now as an old pup!

I hope you enjoy the book, reminiscing and taking a trip down memory lane. I know I will.

Stuart McCall

BRADFORD, EH?

Stuart McCall, Peter Jackson, Bruce Bannister, Dean Richards, Peter Horne, and Dad shone in football, whilst in the '70s, '80s and '90s, I liked sports but never got to the level of such greats.

Bradford produced many great sporting legends, and it wasn't just from football.

Bob Appleyard, David Bairstow, Adil Rashid, Jonny Bairstow, and Harry Brook made their mark in cricket. In the '70s, I tried cricket, but a corky ball busted my nose open, and I retired on Mum's orders.

Yvonne McGregor and Walter Greaves set cycling records. In the '70s and '80s, I was well on my way to setting cycling records of my own. Milk Race? Nah, I didn't win the Milk Race; my record was on how many times a person fell from their Raleigh Chopper. I still have the scars to prove it.

Adrian Moorhouse swam to Olympic glory, and Gavin Meadows picked up four medals in the 1998 Commonwealth Games. In the '80s, I achieved my most outstanding swimming accomplishment: a 50-meter backstroke certificate.

Joe 'The Shoe' Johnson became the snooker world champion in 1986. In the '80s, I managed to make my own record of my highest break of 26 after a year of practice.

In the '90s, in a Bradford pub, I played Andy Appleton, England's pool captain, at pool, and as my memory serves me, I won!

FINAL WORD CREDITS AND SPECIAL THANKS

I hope you enjoyed it half as much as I enjoyed writing it. If you did, I'd really appreciate an honest review. Your feedback means a lot! And if you're after more, I've got another book out:

My Ego Screwed My Acting Career: Based on a True Story—my full autobiography, where I dive into the ups, downs, and all the crazy twists in between.

I will end this book by crediting and thanking the wonderful folk, organisations, and great photographers who were very supportive throughout this journey. Your contributions made a real difference, and I'm deeply grateful. I'm deeply honoured to have the Foreword written by Tasmin Archer and the Afterword by Stuart McCall.

Credits and Special thanks to:

Alice Croot (Mum) for always being supportive

Afterword: Stuart McCall

BRADFORD, EH?

Editor: Lorelli Mojica

Foreword: Tasmin Archer

Front Cover Design: Lorelli Mojica

Front Cover Photo: '80s Westgate in the snow: John Marsh

Geograph Project Ltd

Pennine Radio Jingle and Anecdote: Steve England (Liaison via Simon Prentice).

Permission by Bradford City AFC: Sam Pearce

Permission by Wool Exchange

Permission by St. George's Hall

Photographs supplied and permission granted by the Telegraph & Argus, Bradford: Nigel Burton

School recap: Steve McAleavy

Stencil art photo supplied by creator Stewy

Original images supplied by:

Alan Longbottom, *Gas Conversion 1973*

Alan Murray-Rust, *Odeon Cinema in the City Centre, back in the day, No.16, Prune Park, and Allerton Road, Bradford's last Trolleybus—25 March 1972*

Anne-Lise Heinrichs, *Ay-Ya Ay-Ya Conga*

Betty Longbottom, *Bedford Arms, Wakefield Road, Bradford, Wool Exchange, St. George's Hall, Bradford*

Chris Heaton, *Cartwright Hall*

Christopher Hilton, *Alhambra Theatre in the '90s*

David Grant, *The Pop Man and his van back in the '80s*

Ian Calderwood, *Oops Upside Your Head dance*

Ian Sheppard, *The Cockle Man, back in the day*

BRADFORD, EH?

Janice Staines, *Mill Workers, back in the day*

John Isaacs (D.J. Junk), *'80s Breakdancing*

John Marsh, *Bradford City Centre, back in the day, '70s in the snow, Thornton Road & Westgate '70s Bradford in the snow, steam-hauled trains from Bradford Exchange,'70s Westgate in the snow—Book cover*

John Sutton, *Saltaire: Canal reflections (Salts Mill)*

Justine Gardner, *Jowett cars—Industrial Museum, Sunbridge Wells*

Leonora Enkin, *Corrigan's at Bridlington in the '80s*

Martin Croot, *Various family photos*

Matthew Crowther, *John Street in the '80s, Rackhams' cafe*

Paul Coupland, *Bradford, back in the day*

Paul Hartley, *'90s Night Out*

Paul Sherratt, *Bradford in the '70s*

Pete Hunt, *Elevator Gods Scene*

Richard Thomson, *'70s Gain Lane, snowy winter, St. George's Hall int*

Stephen Craven, *The Wool Exchange int*

Steve Daniels, *Main Street, Haworth. (Brontë Country), Bradford City vs Derby County at Valley Parade, 1982*

Stephen Marland, *Fountains Coffee House, John Street Market, int-ext, back in the day*

St. George's Hall in 1853, Published by Illustrated London News

Stewy, *Polish Anna, stencil art, Oastler Centre, Bradford*

Tasmin Archer, *Headshot*

Terry Walker, *coach (sharra) pulling into Bridlington Station '70s*

Telegraph & Argus Bradford, *Cannon Cinema, Broadway, T & A seller back in the day, Darley Street, Slingsby United team, Stuart McCall 1999*

Printed in Dunstable, United Kingdom

65533727R00068